THE
TEDDY BEAR
JOKE BOOK

Ted E. Bear

Illustrated by Tony Blundell

MAMMOTH

First published in Great Britain 1993
by Mammoth, an imprint of Reed Consumer Books Ltd
Michelin House, 81 Fulham Road, London SW3 6RB
and Auckland, Melbourne, Singapore and Toronto

Text Copyright © 1993 Martyn Forrester
Illustrations copyright © 1993 Tony Blundell

The right of Martyn Forrester to be identified as author
and of Tony Blundell to be identified as illustrator
of this work has been asserted by them in accordance with
the Copyright, Designs and Patents Act 1993

ISBN 0 7497 1412 3

A CIP catalogue record for this title
is available from the British Library

Printed in Great Britain
by Cox & Wyman Ltd, Reading, Berkshire

How do you start a book of teddy
bear jokes?
Say, 'Ready, teddy, go!'

Knock, knock.
Who's there?
Winnie.
Winnie who?
Winnie ya gonna open the door – I've been
knocking for ages!

Knock, knock.
Who's there?
Pooh.
Pooh who?
Don't cry, it's only a joke.

Who's been eating my porridge?' said
Baby Bear.
Who's been eating my porridge?' said
Daddy Bear.
What's all the fuss about?' said Mummy
Bear. 'I haven't made it yet!'

Knock, knock.
Who's there?
Cub.
Cub who?
Cub any closer and you'll catch my code!

Knock, knock.
Who's there?
Furry.
Furry who?
Furry's a jolly good fellow!

Why do some teddy bears in Toyland have
Big Ears?
Because Noddy won't pay the ransom.

7

What famous World War I flying ace was a
teddy bear?
The Red Bear-on.

What do you get if you cross a bear with a
skunk?
Winnie-the-Pooh.

What ghost made friends with the three
bears?
Ghoul-dilocks!

Who's been eating my porridge?' said
Baby Bear.
'Who's been eating my porridge?' said
Mummy Bear.
'Burp!' said Daddy Bear.

What's brown and furry and wears a mask?
The Lone Teddy Bear.

Which teddy bear was a famous rock n' roll singer?
Chuck Beary.

Why didn't Winnie-the-Pooh go outside very much?
He couldn't bear the weather.

Who is a teddy bear's favourite singer?
Beary Manilow.

What's green, comes from Peru, and likes marmalade sandwiches?
Paddington Pear.

Why was Goldilocks from such a small family?
Because she had three bears but everyone else has forebears!

What's green with checked trousers and hangs from trees?
Rupert the Pear.

What's brown and furry, comes from Brazil, and is completely unknown?
Euston Bear.

What do you call a smelly teddy bear?
Winnie-the-Pooh.

Who was brown and furry and wrote lots of famous plays?
William Shakes-bear.

...upert the Bear and Winnie-
... in common?
...name.

...brown and furry and discovered
America?
Christopher Colum-bears.

What do you do if a monster teddy bear
sits in front of you at the cinema watching
'Winnie-the-Pooh'?
Miss most of the film!

Why is Winnie-the-Pooh like Halley's
Comet?
They're both stars with tails.

What do you call a teddy bear at the North Pole?
A teddy brrrrr!

What do you need to spot a polar bear half-a-mile away?
Very good ice-sight.

What's big, white and furry, and found in Liverpool?
A polar bear that's lost.

Where does a two ton polar bear sleep?
Anywhere he wants to!

Did you hear the story about the two polar bears?
Their marriage is on the rocks.

What do you call a polar bear in ear-muffs?
Anything you like, he can't hear you.

What's big, white and furry, and smells of peppermint?
A polo bear.

How can you save money on pet food?
Get a polar bear – they live on ice!

What did the polar bear have for lunch?
Ice-bergers.

How do you get fur from a polar bear?
Run fast in the opposite direction.

Why don't polar bears eat Penguins?
Because they can't get the wrappers off.

'Mummy,' said the baby polar bear, 'am I really, completely, one hundred per cent polar bear?'
'Of course you are, son,' said his mother.
'Why do you ask?'
'Because I'm flipping freezing!'

Why do polar bears have fur coats?
Because they'd look daft in anoraks.

Why don't teddy bears have balls?
Because they can't dance.

What's brown and furry and hovers over your bed?
An Unidentified Flying Teddy Bear.

16

What's brown and furry and drinks from
the wrong side of a glass?
A teddy bear with hiccups.

What do you get if you cross a panda with
a harmonium?
Pandamonium.

What's furry and worn by nudists?
Bear skins.

1ST HUNTER: Have you ever hunted bear?
2ND HUNTER: No, but I've been fishing in my shorts.

What do you get if you cross a grizzly bear with a footballer?
I don't know, but when it goes to score a goal, nobody tries to stop it!

18

What do you get if you cross a grizzly bear with a harp?
A bear-faced lyre.

What do you call a bald teddy bear?
Fred Bear.

What do you call it when two teddys walk around together?
A teddy pair.

What does a teddy say before he goes to bed?
A teddy prayer.

Which side of a teddy bear has more fur?
The outside.

What's brown and furry and always points north?
A magnetic teddy bear.

What's brown and furry and needs no ironing?
A drip-dry teddy bear.

What's brown and furry and goes slam, slam?
A two-door teddy bear.

21

What's brown and furry and good at sums?
A teddy bear with a pocket calculator.

What's brown and furry and bounces?
A teddy bear on a pogo stick.

What's brown and furry and soapy and goes round and round?
A teddy bear in a washing-machine.

What goes out brown and comes back white?
A teddy bear in a snow storm.

What goes out brown and comes back blue?
A teddy bear on a cold day.

What's brown and furry and loves pizza?
An Italian teddy bear.

What did the teddy bear take with him on holiday?
Just the bear essentials.

What do you do with a green teddy bear?
Wait until it ripens.

What did the brown teddy bear say to the blue teddy bear?
'Cheer up!'

What do you call a teddy bear with a machine gun?
Sir!

What is a teddy bear's favourite sport?
The 100 metre cuddle.

What do you call an extra teddy?
A teddy spare.

How do you make a teddy bear fly?
Buy it an airline ticket.

What do you get if you cross a teddy bear
with a pig?
A teddy boar.

What's the difference between a teddy
bear and a biscuit?
*Dunk it in your tea, and if it goes soggy, it's
a biscuit.*

Knock, knock.
Who's there?
Claws.
Claws who?
Claws the window, there's a terrible
draught in here!

What do you call the furry stuff that grows
on a teddy's head?
Teddy hair.

What do you call it when a teddy bear
buys a ticket on the bus?
A teddy fare.

What did the teddy bear say when he was offered a third helping of pudding?
'No thanks, I'm stuffed.'

What is a teddy bear's favourite drink?
Ginger bear.

What disease can teddy bears catch?
Bear-i Bear-i.

What do you call a teddy bear on a golf course?
A golf cub.

What does a teddy bear do before crossing the road?
Paws to look both ways.

What's the best way to catch a teddy bear?
Ask someone to throw it to you.

What's brown and furry, swims in the
ocean, and is very dangerous?
A bear-acuda.

What's brown and furry and has a trunk?
A teddy bear on holiday.

What do teddy bears like for tea?
Cub cakes.

Did you hear the story about Algy and the
bear?
A bear met Algy.
Algy met a bear.
The bear ate Algy.
The bear was bulgy.
The bulge was Algy.

What is a teddy bear's favourite toy?
A Bear-bi doll.

What is a teddy bear's favourite kind of picnic?
A Bear-B-Q.

TED E. BEAR: How do you catch a unique bear?
BUN E. RABBIT: I don't know – how do you?
TED E. BEAR: Unique up on it and grab it!

Why do boy teddy bears wear blue bow-ties?
So you can tell them from girl teddy bears.

What did one teddy bear say to the other teddy bear?
Nothing, silly – teddy bears can't talk.

What do a girl teddy and a boy teddy do if they like each other very much?
They go teddy.

How do you pick up a teddy bear that has been crossed with a porcupine?
Very carefully.

Why is a teddy bear never dressed properly?
Because it always has bear feet.

Why is a teddy bear on the beach like Christmas?
They both have sandy claws (Santa Claus).

Why are teddies always embarrassed?
Because wherever they go, they're always bear.

Why do teddy bears make better friends than crocodiles?
Try cuddling a crocodile and you'll soon find out.

What do you get if you cross a teddy bear with an octopus?
A teddy bear that can cuddle itself.

1ST BEAR: Why is your nose bandaged, teddy?
2ND BEAR: I was smelling a daibsy and got stung by a bee.
1ST BEAR: Not daibsy, teddy – there's no b in daisy.
2ND BEAR: There was in this one!

Fuzzy Wuzzy was a bear,
Fuzzy Wuzzy had no hair.
So Fuzzy Wuzzy wasn't very
Fuzzy, wuzzy?

What kind of weights do teddy bears lift?
Bear-bells.

Once upon a time, in the Wild West, the master of a wagon train was amazed to see a baby teddy bear jump on a horse and gallop off into the distance. Two days later the bear returned. He rode straight up to the wagon master, drew him a map of the ground ahead, and told him the best way to get the wagons through. 'That's amazing,' the wagon master said. 'I've never seen anything like it.' 'You mean to tell me,' the teddy bear said, 'that you've never seen a Cub Scout before?'

What part does a teddy bear usually sing in the chorus?
Bear-itone.

How do teddy bears win races?
Bearly.

Where does a teddy bear get a haircut?
In a bear-ber shop.

What do you call a teddy bear who tried to climb a tree and fell flat on his face in front of his friends?
Em-bear-rassed.

What does a teddy need to breathe?
Teddy air.

What do you call a one-of-a-kind teddy?
A teddy rare.

What do you call a lost teddy?
A teddy where?

What does a teddy get when he treads on
a nail?
A teddy tear.

'I say, your teddy's full of holes.'
'I know, I just don't give a darn.'

Knock, knock.
Who's there?
Fur.
Fur who?
Knock, knock.
Who's there?
Fur.
Fur who?
Knock, knock.
Who's there?
Fur.
Fur who?
Fur heaven's sake, open the door – I've
been knocking for ages.

What is the difference between a teddy
bear?
One of his legs is both the same.

Knock, knock.
Who's there?
Ben.
Ben who?
Ben having picnics in these woods all my life.

What do you get if you cross a teddy bear with peanut butter?
A teddy bear that sticks to the roof of your mouth.

Why did Hannibal go over the Alps with his teddy bear?
Because he couldn't go under them.

Why are some teddy bears such gossips?
They always carry tails with them.

How long should a teddy bear's legs be?
Long enough to reach the ground.

What do you get if you cross ten legs with three tails and a thousand whiskers?
A teddy bear with spare parts.

Why did the girl teddy bear dye her fur yellow?
To see if blondes have more fun.

Why did the teddy bear wear braces?
To keep his trousers up.

What do you get if you cross a teddy bear with a Boy Scout?
Something that's brown and furry and helps old ladies across the road.

Why don't teddy bears ride bicycles?
They don't have thumbs to ring the bell with.

'The police are looking for a lost teddy bear with just one eye.'
'Why don't they use two?'

What is the difference between a teddy bear and an apple?
Have you ever tried peeling a teddy bear?

What is the difference between a teddy bear and a bison?
You can't wash your hands in a teddy bear.

What is the difference between a teddy
bear and an elephant?
*Try picking them up: an elephant is usually
heavier.*

What must a teddy bear be to receive a
state funeral?
Dead.

What do you call a male teddy bear with
ten children?
Daddy.

What do you call a teddy bear that has
written a book?
An author.

What do you call a teddy bear that stuck
its right paw down a lion's throat?
Lefty.

What's brown and furry and swims under
the sea?
A teddy bear with an aqualung.

'Your teddy bear must have three tails.'
'How's that?'
'Well, any teddy bear has more tail than no teddy bear, right? And no teddy bear has two tails, right? So any teddy bear must have three tails!'

When do teddy bears have four feet?
When there are two of them.

What did the man say when he saw one thousand teddy bears come over the hill?
'Here come the teddy bears.'

What did he say when he saw one
thousand teddy bears wearing sunglasses
come over the hill?
Nothing – he didn't recognise them.

What did the dog say to the teddy bear?
'Woof, woof!' (What else?!)

Fifty teddy bears were standing in single
file, all facing the same way. How many of
them could say, 'My nose is touching the
back of another teddy bear's head?'
None – teddy bears can't speak.

Two teddy bears were shipwrecked on an
iceberg. 'Do you think we'll be here long?'
asked the first. 'No,' said the second, 'here
comes the *Titanic.*'

A big, seven-foot tall teddy bear kicks open the saloon door in an old Wild West town. Guns blazing, he drawls to the packed bar: 'Ah've come to get my paw . . .'

Why did the little boy put a teddy bear in his sister's bed?
Because he couldn't find a frog.

How do you make a teddy bear stew?
Keep it waiting for three hours.

Did you hear about the teddy bear with pedestrian eyes?
They look both ways before crossing.

In the fight between the hedgehog and the teddy bear, who won?
The hedgehog won on points.

What goes ha, ha, plop?
A teddy bear laughing its head off.

How do you get two hundred teddy bears in a Mini?
One hundred in the front, one hundred in the back.

How do you get two elephants in a Mini?'
You can't. It's already full up with teddy bears!

How do you get two whales in a Mini?
*Along the M4 and across the Severn
Bridge!* (To Wales – get it?!)

Why did the teddy bear paint itself twenty
different colours?
So it could hide in a box of crayons.

There was a young teddy named Perkins,
Who was so very fond of gherkins;
One day at tea,
He ate fifty-three,
And pickled his internal workings.

Knock, knock.
Who's there?
Thistle.
Thistle who?
Thistle be a perfect day for a teddy bear's
picnic.

Mary had a little ted,
It had a touch of colic;
She gave it brandy twice a day,
And now it's alcoholic.

There was a young teddy from Leeds,
Who swallowed a packet of seeds;
Within just one hour, his nose was a
flower,
And his head was a riot of weeds.

If you saw nine teddy bears sitting at the
cinema with red socks on, and one teddy
bear with yellow socks on, what would that
prove?
*That nine out of ten teddy bears prefer to
wear red socks.*

50

What should you do if a gorilla sits on your favourite teddy bear?
Wait until it gets up again.

What is the difference between a British teddy bear and an American teddy bear?
About three thousand miles.

USA 3,000m.

What's the last thing a teddy bear takes off
when he goes to bed at night?
His feet – off the floor.

What did the teddy bear get on his
birthday?
A year older.

How do you know that pandas are always
fighting?
Because they have two black eyes.

What does a teddy suffer from if he's hit on the head?
A ted-ache.

TEDDY: Doctor, doctor, my hair keeps falling out! What can you give me to keep it in?
DOCTOR: Try this cardboard box.

'If you were walking through the woods and you came across a huge, hungry, angry grizzly bear, would you carry on or would you run back to camp?'
'I'd run back to camp.'
'What – with a bear behind?'

What do you call a really friendy grizzly bear?
A complete failure.

What is a teddy bear's favourite drink?
Coca-Koala.

What do you get if you cross a teddy bear with a vampire?
Something brown and furry that bites you on the neck.

Knock, knock.
Who's there?
Orange.
Orange who?
Orange you glad I'm not a grizzly bear?

What do you call a bear that howls at the moon?
A were-bear.

What's brown and furry and says naughty words?
A swear bear.

What's brown and furry and not very with it?
A square bear.

What's brown and furry and gives you bad dreams?
A night bear.

Why did the teddy bear cross the road?
Because it was the chicken's day off.

Why is a teddy bear's nose in the middle of its face?
Because it's the scenter!

'My teddy has no nose.'
'How does he smell?'
Terrible!'

What do you get when you cross a teddy bear with a skunk?
Rid of the teddy bear!

MAN: Doctor, doctor, you've got to help my brother – he keeps thinking he's a big bear.
DOCTOR: How long has this been going on?
MAN: Ever since he was a cub.

Have you heard about the teddy bear who fell in love with a giraffe?
Well, it's a long story . . .

TEACHER: Spell 'teddy'.
PUPIL: T-e-d-d-d-y.
TEACHER: You'll have to leave out one of the ds.
PUPIL: Which one?

1ST BOY: Has your teddy bear ever had fleas?
2ND BOY: No, only cubs.

1ST GIRL: My teddy comes from South America.
2ND GIRL: Which part?
1ST GIRL: All of him, of course!

'I once saw a teddy that could count.'
'That's nothing, I once saw a spelling bee.'

1ST TEDDY: I've lost my tail. Where can I get another one?
2ND TEDDY: Have you tried a retail shop?

Twenty teddy bears were under a tiny umbrella but none of them got wet. Why not?
It wasn't raining.

'You know Timmy, the boy down the road? He went to college with his teddy bear week after week until the day they parted.'
'You mean he finally left his teddy at home?'
'No, the teddy graduated.'

1ST MAN: I taught my dog to play chess.
2ND MAN: Gosh, he must be terribly clever.
1ST MAN: Not really – I beat him two games out of three.

What's brown and furry on the inside and yellow on the outside?
A teddy bear disguised as a banana.

What's brown and furry with red spots?
A teddy bear with measles.

How many teddy bears can you get in an empty bed?
One – after that, it's not empty any more.

Which teddy bears have the shortest legs?
The smallest ones.

Where do you find most teddy bears?
Between their heads and their feet.

What's brown and furry and lights up?
An electric teddy bear.

What's brown and furry and writes for five miles without stopping?
A ball-point teddy bear.

What is the difference between an egg and a teddy bear?
Ever tried scrambling a teddy bear?

How do you get a teddy bear into a matchbox?
First, you take out all the matches.

'What is the difference between a teddy bear and a matterbaby?'
'What's a matterbaby?'
'Nothing, darling – what's the matter with you?'

Why are teddy bears safe from pickpockets?
They don't have pockets.

'Doctor, doctor, I keep seeing pink teddy bears with yellow spots!'
'Goodness, have you seen a psychiatrist?'
'No, only pink teddy bears with yellow spots.'

What's brown and furry and goes round and round?
A long-playing teddy bear.

What's brown and furry on top, has six legs and two tails, and whinnies?
A teddy bear on a horse.

What's brown and furry and goes thump, squish, thump, squish?
A teddy bear with one wet plimsoll.

What's brown and furry and wears sunglasses?
A teddy bear on holiday.

1ST TEDDY BEAR: My hair is getting thin.
2ND TEDDY BEAR: So what, who wants fat hair?

1ST TEDDY BEAR: How can you avoid falling hair?
2ND TEDDY BEAR: Jump out of the way.

What's yellow and highly cuddly?
Teddy-infested custard.

What's brown and furry and flies a UFO?
A Martian teddy bear.

What's brown and furry and takes
aspirins?
A teddy bear with a headache.

What's brown and furry and travels along
the seabed?
A teddy bear in a submarine.

Who serves the drinks at the teddies'
favourite pub?
The bear-maid.

Why did the teddy bear wear yellow
socks?
*Because his brown ones were at the
laundry.*

What's brown and furry and worn by nudists?
Bear skins.

What's brown and furry and can't keep still?
A teddy bear in a tumble-drier.

How do you make a thin teddy bear fat?
Throw him off a cliff and he'll come down plump!

Why did the teddy bear stop tap dancing?
Because he fell into the sink.

What's brown and furry and goes at 125 mph?
A teddy bear on an Inter-City train.

What do you do if you find one thousand teddy bears in your bed?
Sleep somewhere else.

What do you call a teddy bear that travels First Class in a jumbo jet?
A passenger.

Who is safe when a man-eating teddy bear is on the loose?
Women and children.

When a teddy bear falls into a bath, what is the first thing it does?
Gets wet.

What is the best way to keep teddy bears?
Don't return them.

What did the teddy bear say when the boy
grabbed his tail?
'That is the end of me!'

How can you tell a Spanish teddy bear
from a Scottish one?
By its sun-tan.

How do you tell the difference betwen a
teddy bear and a tin of tomato soup?
Read the label.

Did you hear about the teddy bear with five legs?
His trousers fit him like a glove.

TEACHER: If I had six teddy bears in one hand and six in the other, what would I have?
PUPIL: *Jolly big hands.*

Who is never hungry at Christmas?
The teddy bear – he's always stuffed.

What's brown and furry and hard?
A teddy bear with a machine gun.

Knock, knock.
Who's there?
Hans.
Hans who?
Hans off my honey jar.

Did you hear the story about the
handsome teddy bear?
It's a beautiful tail.

What does a teddy bear grow if he stays
awake long enough?
Tired.

What's brown and furry and flickers?
A teddy bear with a loose connection.

How do teddy bears dress on a cold day?
Quickly.

Where was the teddy bear when his torch
batteries ran out?
In the dark.

Why do some teddy bears wear glasses?
So they don't bump into other teddy bears.

Why do crazy teddy bears eat biscuits?
Because they're crackers.

What do you call a teddy bear with a
banana in each ear?
Anything you like – he can't hear you.

74

'What is your favourite colour?'
'Purple.'
'And what is your favourite cuddly toy?'
'A teddy bear.'
And what is your favourite number?'
'Seven.'
'So when did you last see a purple teddy
bear with seven legs?'

Why should you never listen to a teddy
bear in bed?
Because he's lying.

Which teddy bear wears the biggest hat?
The one with the biggest head.

Do teddy bears snore?
Only when they're asleep.

Why did the teddy bear cut the legs off his
bed?
Because he wanted to lie low for a while.

What's the difference between a teddy
bear and a biscuit?
It's hard to dunk a teddy bear in your tea.

Why did the stupid teddy bear take a
pencil to bed?
Because he wanted to draw the curtains.

What's brown and furry and noisy?
A teddy bear with a drum kit.

What is brown and furry and travels
around your bed at 100 mph?
A teddy bear on a motorbike.

What do you get if you cross a river with an inflatable teddy bear?
To the other side.

BOY AT LOST PROPERTY OFFICE: I'm looking for a teddy bear with one eye called Cuddles.
LOST PROPERTY MAN: What's his other eye called?

'My daughter has just got an Irish teddy bear.'
'Oh really?'
'No, O'Reilly.'

Why was the teddy bear glad that everyone called him Mr Softy?
Because that was his name.

What's brown and furry and weighs two tons?
A very fat teddy bear.

What is the best way to get a wild teddy bear?
Buy a tame one and irritate it.

'How many teddy bears are there in a hammerfor?'
'What's a hammerfor?'
'Banging in nails!'

What do you get if you cross a teddy bear's brain with a piece of elastic?
A stretch of the imagination.

Why did the teddy bear sleep in a cardboard box?
Because the council wouldn't give him a flat.

How can you tell a teddy bear from spaghetti?
A teddy bear doesn't fall off the end of your fork.

How do you make a teddy bear float?
Take two scoops of ice cream and add one teddy bear.

What makes more noise than an angry teddy bear?
Two angry teddy bears.

Why do teddy bears lie down at night?
Because they can't lie up.

Why didn't the teddy bear hurt itself when it fell off the ladder?
It only fell from the bottom rung.

Why is a teddy bear brown and furry?
So you can tell it from your pillow.

TEDDY BEAR: Doctor, Doctor, I'm only thirty centimetres tall.
DOCTOR: You'll just have to be a little patient.

What is teddy bear fur used for most?
To keep teddy bears together.

How do you stop a teddy bear from smelling?
Cut off its nose.

Why does a teddy bear wear sandals?
To go to the beach.

When should a bear carry an umbrella?
When it's raining cats and dogs.

What looks like half a teddy bear?
The other half.

1ST TEDDY BEAR: Where do you sleep?
2ND TEDDY BEAR: On a chandelier.
1ST TEDDY BEAR: Why's that?
2ND TEDDY BEAR: Because I'm a light sleeper.

What's brown and furry and sees as well from either end?
A teddy bear with its eyes shut.

What do you have to know to teach a
teddy bear tricks?
More than the teddy bear.

'I bet I can make you forget about the giant
man-eating teddy bear.'
'What giant man-eating teddy bear?'
'See – you've forgotten already.'

What do you give a seasick teddy bear?
Plenty of room!

What do you call a girl teddy bear with only one leg?
Eileen.

How can you tell if there's a monster teddy bear in the food cupboard?
By the footprints in the honey jar.

Why wouldn't the teddy bear jump off the top diving-board?
Because he didn't have the guts.

Why do teddy bears live in children's beds?
Because the rent is low.

What's brown and smells?
A teddy bear's nose.

Where do the cleanest teddy bears live?
Bath.

What do you call a teddy bear that lies on the floor all the time?
Matt.

KID TEDDY BEAR: Mum, am I made of sage and onion?
MOTHER TEDDY BEAR: Of course not. Why?
KID TEDDY BEAR: Because a big teddy bear from the end of the street said he's going to knock the stuffing out of me.

What happened to the teddy bear that ran away with the circus?
The police made him bring it back.

How can you tell if there's a monster teddy
bear under your bed?
If your face is nearly touching the ceiling.

Did you hear about the teddy bear that fell
into a barrel of beer?
He came to a bitter end.

What's the difference between an injured
teddy bear and bad weather?
*One roars with pain, the other pours with
rain.*

The bear stood on the bridge one night,
Its fur was all a-quiver;
It gave a cough,
Its leg fell off,
And floated down the river.

How can you tell if there's a monster teddy
bear in your bed?
By the T on his pyjamas.

What do you call a teddy bear that's fallen
into the bath and can't swim?
Bob.

What do you get if you cross a teddy bear
with a pig?
Furry pork chops.

How can you tell if a teddy bear has a
glass eye?
If it comes out in conversation.

How can you tell if the world's largest
teddy bear is hiding in your fridge?
The door won't close.

What kind of teddy bears have their eyes
closest together?
The smallest ones.

Why is hunting for honey like a legacy?
Because it is a bee-quest.

What's brown and furry, makes honey, and
is hard to understand?
A mumble bee.

What did the bee say to the flower?
'Hello, honey.'

88

Why do bees fly around crossing and uncrossing their legs?
They're looking for a BP station.

What did the mother bee say to the baby bee?
'Don't be naughty, honey, just beehive while I comb your hair.'

Why do bees have sticky hair?
Because they have honey combs.

Why do bees hum?
Because they don't know the words.

What goes zzub, zzub?
A bee flying backwards.

What do bees do with honey?
They cell it.

What are the bees on strike for?
More honey and shorter flowers.

What do bees say in summer?
'Swarm!'

What's brown and furry and highly
dangerous?
*A hand grenade disguised as a teddy
bear.*

JOHN: I've got a teddy bear that can
count.
AMY: Is that so?
JOHN: Yes, I asked him what two minus
two was and he said nothing.

How do teddy bears watch Neigh-bears?
On teddy-vision.

Which airport do teddy bears fly from when
they go on their holidays?
Stans-Ted.

What did one teddy bear say when
another teddy bear told him a joke?'
'Furry funny.'

What's brown and furry and goes put-put-
put?
An outboard teddy bear.

What's brown and furry and goes splutter-
splutter-splutter?
*An outboard teddy bear running out of
petrol.*

What's brown and furry, has one bionic
eye, and fights crime?
The Six Million Dollar Teddy Bear.

MAN: Can I have a teddy bear for my son, please?
TOY SHOP OWNER: *I'm sorry, sir, we don't do swaps.*

TEDDY BEAR: Us teddy bears are much smarter than you chickens.
CHICKENS: *Oh, yeah? And what makes you say that?*
TEDDY BEAR: Ever seen Kentucky Fried Teddy Bear?

Why do teddy bears have brown and furry necks?
To connect their heads to their bodies.

How do you make a teddy fly?
Start with a furry zip.

'How is a skunk different from a teddy bear?'
'I don't know. How?'
'A skunk uses cheaper deodorant.'

What's green and furry?
A seasick teddy bear.

TOM: What's brown and furry and made of cement?
FINBAR: What?
TOM: A teddy bear.
FINBAR: But what about the cement?
TOM: I just threw that in to make it hard.

What do you get if you cross a hyena with Winnie-the-Pooh?
An animal that laughs at its own teddy bear jokes!

What do you get if you cross a teddy bear with a giraffe?
An animal that cuddles low-flying aircraft.

What do teddy bears have that no other animal has?
Baby teddy bears.

Why don't you ever see teddy bears in the zoo?
Because they can't afford the admission.

What is a teddy bear's favourite breakfast cereal?
Teddy Brek.

What did the policeman say to the three-headed teddy bear?
'Hello, hello, hello.'

What's brown and furry inside, white outside, and difficult to eat?
A teddy bear sandwich.